to make you

Puke

Tulip Kilbourne

Illustrations by
Scott Vanden Bosch

 **blue cat** books

First published in 2000 by blue cat books
www.users.bigpond.net.au/bluecatbooks

Text © Tulip Kilbourne
Illustrations © Scott Vanden Bosch

National Library of Australia
Cataloguing-in-Publication entry

Kilbourne, Tulip.
Poems to make you puke.
ISBN O-646-39979-9.

I. Title.

A821.4

Designed by Lee Lewis
Printed in Australia by Australian Print Group

Distributed nationally by Dennis Jones & Associates
and in New Zealand through Addenda Limited

**If you have a weak stomach
do not turn these pages.**

YOU'VE BEEN WARNED!

For the Tinker's Daughter
and Sister Golden-Hair   (T.K.)

For Emma, Amy and Magic (S.V.B.)

Contents

Chunder Challenge

These are the most disgusting rhymes
They'll make you wanna puke at times
So keep a bucket next to you
In case you get the urge to spew

But if you think you're tough enough
To swallow all this yucky stuff
Go ahead and read right through
And try your hardest not to spew

And if by some amazing luck
You make it through without a chuck
You'll be crowned the Prince of Hurl
Or Queen of Puke, if you're a girl

But if your tummy's pretty weak
You're not advised to take a peek
Don't even have the smallest look
Just go and read a baby book

My Sister

My sister is a spoilt brat
Demanding this, demanding that!
I hate that little whining punk
I'd love to push her off our bunk

I'll fix that girl, here's what I'll do
I'll fill her bed with tonnes of spew
I'll spread around all nice and thick –
Stacks and stacks of chunky sick!

Full of half-chewed carrots and peas
Sick that stinks like smelly cheese
What a plan! No room for blunder
But where am I gonna get the chunder?

That's okay, no need to grieve
I've heaps of plans stuck up my sleeve
I'll wait until she's gone to bed
Then wipe some boogers on her head

I hope they're soft, not hard to pick
Hard ones won't stick unless you lick
Hard or soft, I'll fill her dimples
So they look like bright green pimples

I'll drop some frogs into her bath
And she'll get warts – now that's a laugh!
Warts on her legs, how very rotten
I hope she gets them on her bottom

If that won't work, here's what I'll try
I'll bake sweet sis' an apple pie
Instead of apples burning hot
I'll fill the pie with heaps of snot

I'm gonna get that little twit
But if Mum finds out she'll chuck a fit
She'll say, 'Be nice now, she's your sis'
Best make up – give her a kiss.'

Yuck! How gross, I'd rather die
I'd rather kiss a mouldy fly
Anything but kiss that cow
I might put off my plans . . . for now!

Dear Santa

Dear Santa Claus, I think you stink
I'd like to paint your beard bright pink
Squeeze your jingle bells real hard
And tear up all your Christmas cards

Santa, you're a lazy slob
You cannot even do your job
You only have to work one night
And you can't even get that right!

Where's my Barbie and my bike?
I never asked you for a trike
I'm all grown up now, can't you see –
I need two wheels, I don't need three!

You've brought me lots of brand new clothes
Now what's a kid to do with those?
You cannot play with shirts or socks
And what fun is a pair of jocks?

And, Santa, where's my basketball?
I wanted that the most of all
Now what am I supposed to throw?
Christmas balls don't bounce you know

I asked you for a Cabbage Patch
You promised me you'd bring a batch
But not one doll – that's so unfair!
Just heaps and heaps of underwear

Santa Claus, you are no good –
You eat too much Christmas pud
Your stomach's such a massive roll
You must have high cholesterol

I bet you never make the gifts
But get the elves to work the shifts
Then you lay back in the sleigh
While reindeer pull you all the way

I'm sending these dumb presents back
And you can shove them in your sack
Next Christmas, Santa, I insist
You'd better double-check your list

And if you get it wrong next year
I'll come and holler in your ear
I'll shove some tinsel up your nose
And melt some candles on your toes

I'll get a pack of dogs – you'll see –
To piddle up your Christmas tree
I'll tip your pudding on your head
And put a snowman in your bed

So that is all I have to say
And, oh yeah, Santa, by the way
Merry Christmas, lots of cheer
See you Christmas time next year

Eating Worms

Mum says I'll get stacks of germs
If I keep eating garden worms
I eat them coated thick with dirt
I'm sure a little dirt won't hurt

One day Mum got really flustered
'Cause I stuck worms into my custard
She thought that it was poor behaviour
But I just wanted extra flavour

She said, 'Listen here, you must behave!'
But I zapped some in the microwave
I must have set it way too high –
You should've seen the worm-guts fly!

Mum said, 'No more worms on your agenda!'
But I tossed a handful in the blender
'Cause worm thick-shakes are quite a treat
They're full of blood and minced worm meat

She said, 'Enough, now that will do!'
But I threw some on the barbecue
You should've seen poor Aunty Kate
As wiggly worms crawled on her plate!

So Mum dug worms with all her might
She dug all day, and dug all night
Then she flushed them down the loo
She said, 'Well, fishies like worms too.'

But, hey that's cool, I'd had enough
I thought I'd try some other stuff
I made myself an apple cider
And dropped in one big hairy spider

It was yummy, soft yet firm
And tasted just a bit like worm

The Very Hairy, Scary Fairy

Last night I saw something scary
Above my bed was a mean tooth fairy
She was big and fat and hairy –
A very hairy, scary fairy!

Beneath an eye she had a bruise
And up her arms she had tattoos
Half her teeth had fallen out
Poo! She smelt like a brussels sprout

She yelled, 'Hey, Ugly, open wide
I need to take a look inside.'
Then she gave a wicked grin
And tried to kick my front teeth in

She screamed, 'I want your teeth right now!'
I said, 'They're mine you stupid cow –
My teeth are staying in my head!'
And then I shoved her off the bed

But in my mouth that fairy flew
She was tough and hard to chew
'I'll take them all!' I heard her shout
I quickly spat that fat thing out

I said, 'Hey, don't you know the rules –
Don't they have tooth fairy schools?
You only get my teeth, you see
Once they've fallen out of me

'Then I put them in a glass
And you can fetch them as you pass
Of course there'll be a little fee
At least two coins or maybe three.'

She said, 'Listen here you nincompoop
Listen close 'cause here's the scoop –
I want some teeth, I want them now
I don't care whose, I don't care how.'

I said, 'Fairy, I have plans –
I think you should go to my Nan's
'Cause every night, without a doubt
Nana takes her false teeth out.'

She looked intrigued, until I said
'They're in some water by her bed.'
She sat down and cried and cried
'I can't swim, but how I've tried!'

I said, 'I'll teach you how to swim.'
I grabbed a glass and threw her in
'Be sure to hold your breath,' I said
But she just sunk and soon was dead

So today I thought I'd bake
A nice big juicy fairy cake

Dog Poo

When I was walking through the park
I stood on something soft and dark
I took a whiff of my right shoe
And sure enough I smelt dog poo!

I let out one almighty scream –
'Ahhh! It's fresh – check out the steam!'
Fresh doggy-dos the worst, I thought
Why wasn't this the dried out sort?

I tried to wipe it off my shoe
But this poo stuck like super glue
I tried to scrape it on a rock
And somehow spread it on my sock

Then I spied a drinking-tap
And went to wash off all that crap
But that just made some parents frown –
You'd think I'd pulled my trousers down!

This was the most resilient bog
If only I could find that dog
I wouldn't yell, I wouldn't hit –
I'd make him lick off every bit

My Pink Shoes

My favourite shoes are lipstick pink
They look so nice, but they sure stink!
If I'm around, you'd wheeze and cough
Should I decide to kick them off

I always stamp and scream and pout
Whenever Mum says, 'Throw them out!'
'I love my shoes,' I proudly yell
'And so what if they kind of smell.'

But last night when I went to sleep
Mum threw them on the rubbish heap
When I woke up Mum said, 'Bad luck!
Your shoes are in that garbage truck.'

She said, 'Those shoes were getting old
Scuffed and growing specks of mould.'
'You're old too,' I blurted out
'But no one tries to throw you out!'

I was mad and blew a fuse
I thought I'd go and find my shoes
I grabbed my bag and zipped the zip
Then headed off towards the tip

I searched through piles of old car tyres
Rags and clothes and chicken wires
Orange peel, banana skins
Piles of muck from dirty bins

There were heaps of yucky smells
Slimy stuff in cracked eggshells
Smoke butts, teabags dripping wet
But not one sign of my shoes yet

I searched for ages through that stuff
'Til that was it, I'd had enough
I was sick of all that stink
But then I spotted something pink

Stuck beneath some cold spaghetti
Dried out leaves and used confetti
Cotton reels and broken zippers
I thought I'd found my favourite . . . slippers!

Slippers! Slippers! What a twit –
They weren't my shoes, but they sure fit
I snuck those slippers in my pack
Then turned around to head on back

But something pinkish caught my eye
Sticking out of mouldy pie
Fishbone, wishbone, old grapefruits
There they were my favourite . . . boots!

30

They weren't my shoes, though they were cool
I thought I'd wear those boots to school
When I got home my bag was chockers
Man, my mum went off her rocker!

'They're disgusting – take them back!'
I said, 'Don't have a spack-attack!
Sure they smell, but not that bad
I've smelt worse smells come out of Dad.'

Mum just gave a wicked stare
Until I took back every pair
I dumped the lot, the pink boots too
And headed home without one shoe

But on my bed was something pink –
Brand new shoes that didn't stink!
Just like the ones that Mum threw out
My favourite shoes without a doubt

Mum came in and gave a wink
'They smell much nicer, don't you think?'
'Thanks so much, they're great,' I said
And wore my brand new shoes to bed

Smelly Babies

Babies are d-i-s-g-u-s-t-i-n-g critters
They whinge, they cry, they are food spitters
Some people say they look so sweet
I think they look like lumps of meat

Babies smell and are quite happy
To sit there in a pooey nappy
It can trickle down their legs
So if you're near one wear a peg

Wear it firmly on your nose
And never wear your bestest clothes
Babies have been known to spew –
They're bound to do it all down you!

My parents bought one from the hossie
It can't talk, but it's sure bossy
It screams and screams when it wants food
And looks disgusting in the nude

It's just not fair that little mite
Gets to snack all through the night
If I snuck snacks, I'd be in trouble –
'Get back to bed now on the double!'

Babies never talk or walk
They just eat, poo, spew and squawk
They're horrid things, so what's the point?
Who needs a baby round the joint?

I think I'll swap ours for a bunny
Or maybe I'll get back our money
But, 'No refunds,' the nurse reported
'Once they're home that's it!' she snorted

So I put an ad in Friday's Mail –

ONE ALMOST BRAND NEW BABY

FOR SALE

Barely used, it's in good nick

Just fifty cents

You'd best be quick!

Mrs Cowbreath up the road
Nearly bought the grotty toad
But she's a witch – I know it's true –
She'd mince it up for baby stew

Dribbling babies aren't my style
They're grotty, gross, extremely vile
But my mum says it's got my smile
So we might keep it . . . for a while!

The Boys' Toilets

I wonder what's behind those walls
Where males go when nature calls?
I really think it's so unfair
That girls are not allowed in there!

At least a hundred times I've tried
But boys won't let me go inside
I reckon they have gum machines
And walls made out of jellybeans

Shelves stacked full of chocolate milk
And toilet paper soft as silk
And toilet bowls that sing and dance
While pulling up your underpants

I reckon as you wash your hands
You'd hear a tune from marching bands
And then the taps would fill the sink
With lemonade for you to drink!

My friend says that I've got it wrong
She says boys' toilets really pong
She says one day she snuck inside
And when she sniffed she nearly died

She says that it was pretty scary
The toilet bowls were really hairy
They had fangs beneath their lids
To chew up any naughty kids

She said one boy was in a rush
So much so he didn't flush
The toilet turned him into mince
And no one's seen that poor boy since

She says the toilet rolls were bare
No toilet paper – not one square!
And so it seems, she now believes
Boys wipe their bums upon their sleeves

One day soon I'll take a squizz
At where the boys all take a whiz
And then I'll finally know for sure
What hides behind those toilet doors

Pop's Piles

Pop has piles and piles of things
Piles of toe nails, piles of strings
Piles of cats all mouldy and dead
Piles of chewy stuck to his bed

Piles of broccoli starting to smell
Piles of pears and maggots as well
Piles of pizza older than you
Piles of unflushed goo in the loo

Piles of snails he found on the path
Piles of worms he keeps in the bath
Piles of spiders he stores in a tin –
To open up when the kiddies come in

Piles of slugs that sit on the couch
Piles of bugs in a yucky old pouch
Piles of ear wax stuck to the telly
Piles of flies in raspberry jelly

Piles of socks that don't seem to match
Piles of lice eggs waiting to hatch
Piles of clothes on the bedroom floor –
Too smelly to wear – so Pop's in the raw

Piles and piles of rubbish that stink
Piles of dishes stacked in the sink
Piles of chunder where Pop was sick
He ran to the toilet, but isn't that quick!

A pile of bones that used to be Nan
She died while eating a pile of bran
She fell to the ground in a neat little pile
And that's where she stayed – now isn't that vile!

Piles of dog poo around the backyard
That's been there so long it's gone white and hard
Pop loves his piles – in fact when he's dead
He wants to be left in a pile on his bed

Squished

I had a pet – a big fat cat –
But late last week I heard a splat
Puss was hit by a speeding car
And made a dent in the bumper bar

I scraped some squished bits off the tyre
Its brains were up a little higher
Mum said, 'Put it in the bin!'
But I kept puss in a biscuit tin

I sometimes get it out to play
'Cause I can't throw poor puss away
It doesn't meow or eat a lot
And never has to lick its bot

Sure it smells much worse than poo
And all those maggots make me spew
But I still like to stroke its fur
Just in case I make puss purr

Challenge Check

So did you gasp here and there?
Then chuck your guts up everywhere?
Or are you one of just a few
To make it through without a spew?

Well, if you made it, you're a freak
Most kids' stomachs are too weak
You're hereby crowned the Prince of Hurl
Or Queen of Puke, if you're a girl

About the Author

Not a great deal is known about this funky flower of chuck, Tulip Kilbourne, except that she is delicate, rare and elusive. Perhaps this is quite enough!

About the Illustrator

Scott Vanden Bosch is a talented animator and illustrator. He shares his studio with robots, sea monsters and a leaky roof.

Find out more
http://www.users.bigpond.net.au/bluecatbooks